START BEING
VISIBLE

The best opportunities

come to those who are visible.

START BEING VISIBLE

VISIBLE

Raise your profile, promote your brand, and attract your ideal clients – through LinkedIn!

MILDRED TALABI

DEDICATION

*This book is dedicated to all the women
who have ever struggled with being visible online.*

The world is ready and waiting to see you.

Your time is now.

Much love x

CONTENTS

INTRODUCTION

IF YOU'VE PICKED UP THIS BOOK, it's probably because you have a business aimed at professionals and you've tried other social media platforms and found that they're not quite cutting it when it comes to connecting you with your target audience.

You've heard people tell you that LinkedIn is the place to be for your business, but you still have some doubts as to whether you can actually get tangible results from the time you spend on this platform.

And, if we're being really honest, there's a small part of you that's a little afraid of putting yourself "out there" on LinkedIn. You know it's important for you to be visible but the idea of showing up and sharing your real self is a little intimidating – I mean, how will people react, right?

I've been where you are.

I ran my previous business, CV Makeover Expert, for 12 years and during the latter half of this time, I overcame my fears of being visible and used LinkedIn as the primary source to promote my brand and build my business.

Prior to that, I trained as a journalist, worked in a few newspapers and magazines and later transitioned into Public Relations (PR) and Communications.

Both my time in the media and my time in business has taught me that being visible is foundational to your business success. You can have the best business in the world but if nobody sees or hears from you, they won't buy from you. You need to be visible so you can easily promote your brand and effortlessly attract your ideal clients.

And what better place to do this online than on LinkedIn.

LinkedIn is the biggest professional platform in the world and the opportunities to find and connect with your target audience there are endless so it's a no-brainer, especially if you have a service-based business.

Through being visible on LinkedIn, I've been paid to speak to a wide variety of audiences. I've featured in newspapers and magazines, been interviewed on podcasts and radio shows, and I've even appeared on television.

Over the next few chapters, we will go into more detail on why visibility is important and why LinkedIn is the best platform to achieve this for your business. I will walk you through the four pillars of LinkedIn success (profile, content, engagement and audience) and how you can implement these pillars to build your brand and grow your business through LinkedIn.

WHAT THIS BOOK IS NOT…

What you won't get with this book is the boring nuts and bolts of LinkedIn.

You're not going to find heavy technical descriptions on things like LinkedIn algorithm (though they do get a mention) and you're not going to get a blow-by-blow account of every feature on LinkedIn since, as is the nature of the fast-paced world of social media, this is likely to change and be out of date by the time the ink is dry on this paper.

However, what I do promise is that if you stick with me and read and apply everything I share with you in this book, you will fast-track your journey to LinkedIn visibility and be well on your way to business success.

So, if you're ready, let's dive in!

CHAPTER 1

WHY BE VISIBLE?

HERE'S THE THING – you could be the absolute best at what you do in your business but if no one knows about it, it won't do you (or them) any good so they won't hire you.

Being visible is about being seen, being heard and being remembered by the people you are looking to serve with your products or services.

It's about elevating your profile and your brand to the place where you are now seen by your clients and peers as someone who has expertise in your niche area and provides great knowledge and value.

Being visible exposes you to interesting people and opportunities, sometimes well outside your scope of expectations.

Being visible can help you get more clients for your business, make more money and have a better life. It can also provide you with a platform and the influence to advocate for causes close to your heart and make an impact in people's lives in this way.

If being visible has so many advantages, why do so many people shy away from it?

To answer that question takes us to the connection being visible has with your personal brand.

VISIBILITY AND YOUR PERSONAL BRAND

The starting place with being visible is to understand a little more about the concept of your personal brand and how this works.

We all have a personal brand, whether we know it or not. If you're in a service business – particularly if you are a solopreneur – your personal brand matters even more because people don't just buy your services, they buy into *you*!

Once people know you can solve their problem, the next thing they want to know is who you are as a human being, to help them decide if they can work with you.

You are the face of your brand so it's important for you to become visible in order to humanise and sustain your business.

Being visible helps people understand what you do and what you stand for. It's how they get to know, like and trust your brand.

THE FEAR OF BEING VISIBLE

In the course of my business as a LinkedIn Visibility Coach, I've spoken to many business owners (mainly women) about their reasons for not being more visible on LinkedIn and one of the reasons that keep coming up time and time again is the issue of fear – the fear of being visible.

Being visible can be uncomfortable at best and downright scary at worst, so that's totally understandable.

There's the fear of saying the wrong thing; the fear of being judged or criticised; the fear of looking bad; the fear of not coming across as an expert (the impostor syndrome); the fear of annoying people by showing up too much...and much more!

In order to start being visible, you need to let go of these fears. You need to be willing to be seen and heard so you can be remembered and hired.

If it helps, think back to why you started your business in the first place. Yes, it is to provide a service that helps people, but what were the personal benefits for you? Is it to create more income so you can spend more time travelling? Is it to have the flexibility to spend time with your spouse? Is it so you can see your children more and be more involved in their school life? Whatever the reason was and is, being visible will help you achieve that goal.

VISIBILITY – A BUSINESS-GROWING TOOL

Being visible is an important tool to grow your business. You must be visible to attract a consistent flow of clients. If nobody knows you, you can't help anyone.

You want to aim to be so visible that you take up residence in the minds of your ideal clients so that they will forever associate you with your services and remember you when they need support in that area.

To do this, you need to show up constantly and consistently and share, share and share your message. Latest research suggests that it now takes an average of 15-21 times for us to hear a message before it truly registers in our minds. Always assume your target audience have yet to hear your message and take every opportunity you can to get it in front of them.

Also, only around 40% of LinkedIn users are active on a regular basis, which means there is a real opportunity for you to rise above your peers and claim that top space in your field – and all the benefits that come along with it – by being visible.

STRATEGIC VISIBILITY

As you start to get into the habit of showing up regularly on LinkedIn and being visible, you will start to see that there are some people who appear to be online all day long, posting content and engaging with people, but in reality they've mastered the art of strategic visibility – showing up when it counts and showing up often enough so it counts.

I once had a conversation with a prospective client and in the conversation she said, "I reached out to you because it got to the point that every time I opened up my LinkedIn, I knew I was guaranteed to see a post from you on my feed without fail. I want to be *that* visible to my target audience!"

Strategic visibility is a good practice to get into, especially if you're pressed for time, as most business people are, and haven't got all day to be on LinkedIn.

How it works is that you show up on LinkedIn for short blocks of time throughout the day. For example, you can clock in 20 minutes in the morning when you post your content and carry out some early engagement; at lunchtime you can schedule in another 15 minutes of engagement, responding to inbox messages and so on, and then do the same again for another 15 minutes in the evening.

Not only does this technique of strategic visibility allow you to have major impact in less than an hour of LinkedIn use a day, it also allows you to engage with connections across different time zones who are waking up at different times during the day – and when you do this, it looks like you're always online and always visible.

A NOTE ON AUTHENTICITY

Authenticity is something that often comes up in discussions around being visible on social media. It's become one of those buzzwords everyone uses or wants to be associated with.

In a society where we are trusting the official channels and voices less and less, everyone is looking for that "authentic" personality or brand to follow. At the same time, we're being encouraged by "experts" to be more authentic in the way we show up online.

But what does it actually mean to be authentic? My very simple definition is this – being the same person online as you are offline. When you're authentic in the way you show up on LinkedIn, the right people – your audience – will be drawn to you. Others will be repelled, and that's a good thing.

Your personality or style of communication will put people off and that is not only okay, but desirable! You only want to work with people that like you for you anyway!

CHAPTER 2

WHY LINKEDIN?

AT THE TIME OF WRITING, LinkedIn is the world's largest professional networking site, with a reported 706 million active users on the platform.

Although most people still think of LinkedIn as a place to find jobs, LinkedIn is so much more than that and has evolved – and continues to evolve – over the years.

LinkedIn is a great platform if you want to be a thought leader in your industry. It's an excellent place to gain visibility, demonstrate your business expertise, and create valuable discussions within your community.

Being visible on LinkedIn is an essential way to establish credibility in your field, expand your network, and attract ideal clients into your business.

LINKEDIN IS **NOT** A "PROFESSIONAL" PLATFORM

Although LinkedIn is the number one professional networking platform, when it comes to thinking about how to use it to raise your visibility, it's important to lose that idea to a certain extent.

I've spoken to lots of business owners over the years who would do so well on LinkedIn but they've been reluctant to engage with the platform because they believe that LinkedIn is a "professional" platform – and for them that means you either show up officially, dressed to the nines (metaphorically), or you don't show up at all.

If your reason for not wanting to be visible on LinkedIn is because you're afraid you might not come across as "professional" enough if you show up with your authentic self, let me set you free with some truth – LinkedIn is not a "professional" platform!

Sure, there are plenty of people on LinkedIn looking to do business or find jobs; and sure, you're likely to get the virtual equivalent of a stern look if you relentlessly post videos about your cat or your cute kids, but at its core LinkedIn, like any other platform, is filled with people. And guess what? People buy from people, not from "professionals".

There's more than enough space for you to show up as yourself on LinkedIn – in fact, this is majorly important if you plan on using LinkedIn to promote your brand and attract your ideal clients.

PEOPLE BUY FROM PEOPLE – SOCIAL SELLING AND RELATIONSHIP BUILDING

You've probably come across the term "social selling" before.

At its most basic, social selling is the idea and practice of 'selling' to people through social media platforms.

If we elaborate on it a little more, social selling is the practice of using social media to find, connect with, understand, develop and nurture meaningful relationships with your target audience so you become the first person they think of when they want to buy what you're selling.

Social selling is not about incessantly sharing links about your business in your posts or in LinkedIn groups. It's also not about sending people unsolicited inbox messages on LinkedIn about your services, and it's definitely not about stealing the email address of your LinkedIn connections and adding them to your business mailing list without permission.

If you've been on LinkedIn for any length of time you've probably found yourself at the receiving end of at least one of these malpractices.

People who carry out this type of activity probably genuinely believe they are "marketing", but what they are actually doing is spamming, and no one likes that. These kinds of practices irritate and alienate people, as well as discredit the businesses involved. Stay well away from them.

Social selling is about selling without *selling*. The truth is people like to buy but they don't like to be sold to. Social selling is about presenting yourself and your business as the solution to the most pressing problems your target audience face.

When you do social selling well through being visible, you become attractive to your ideal clients. Instead of you having to chase them down through cold calling (or cold messaging) and other hardcore sales tactics, your ideal clients will be *drawn* to you and will take the initiative to approach *you* to engage your services.

Social selling, through building and maintaining relation-ships with your target audience, is a relatively painless sales technique, compared to the dreaded cold outreach, but one that yields great results. To do well at social selling you need to genuinely put the needs of your target audience before your own and seek to serve them by meeting their needs and addressing their pain points.

THE FOUR PILLARS OF SOCIAL SELLING

LinkedIn is the ideal platform to implement social selling strategies. According to the site itself, there are four pillars to effective social selling via its platform and these are:

1. Create a strong professional brand

2. Find and connect with your target audience

3. Share relevant content relating to your field

4. Build trusted relationships with your target audience through helpful content and genuine conversations

LinkedIn has also gone a step further to quantify the value of social selling by creating its own unique measurement sys-tem, called the Social Selling Index (SSI).

MEASURING YOUR SSI SCORE

The Social Selling Index is scored on a scale of 0 – 100 based on how well you carry out the four pillars of social selling on LinkedIn.

Though aimed at sales professionals (as it's designed to work alongside LinkedIn's Sales Navigator offering – more on this later), the SSI score is a great way to measure the impact of your activities on Linkedin, even if you're not in sales (although as a business person, you are *always* in the business of sales!).

The SSI score is also a visibility measure to a certain extent. LinkedIn has found a strong correlation between those who achieve their sales goals and those who have a high SSI score, with 70 and above being the golden number to aim for.

In essence, the more visible you are on LinkedIn (through implementing LinkedIn's four pillars of social selling and carrying out the activities covered in this book), the higher your SSI score will be; and the higher your SSI score, the more business and other opportunities you will attract your way.

You can find your score by visiting www.linkedin.com/sales/ssi.

Although helpful, the SSI score is only a guideline, so don't get obsessed with checking your number on a regular basis –

it's far more important to focus on actually *doing* the things that lead to increasing your score.

THE LAW OF 'SEEDTIME AND HARVEST'

Have you heard of the concept of 'seedtime and harvest'?

It's a Biblical concept but also a farming analogy and a life principle which suggests that in order to reap a harvest of any kind, you need to first plant the seeds.

Farmers have an allocated time (a season) for planting seeds in their field and they have an allocated time to return to those fields and collect the harvest. If a farmer wants to grow corn, he first plants corn seeds into the ground, leaves it for a period of time, and then returns later to collect the harvest of corn.

LinkedIn works in much the same way. If you want to use LinkedIn to raise your profile, promote your brand and attract your ideals, you need to employ the process of seedtime and harvest.

You plant the seeds of applying the four pillars of LinkedIn success you will learn in this book, and you reap the harvest of visibility, brand recognition and client attraction.

However, it's important to highlight the small four-letter word wedged in between the 'seedtime and harvest' phrase, and that word is *time.*

LinkedIn is *not* for you if you want overnight success.

It takes time to reap a harvest.

It takes time to raise your visibility, build your personal brand and establish your credibility.

It takes time for people to know you, like you and trust you. It takes time for the momentum to build and for opportunities to start to come your way through your activities on LinkedIn.

But if you continue to plant the right seeds, and you remain patient and consistent over time, you will surely reap a harvest – just as surely as the farmer who plants corn seeds gets corn crops.

Don't try and rush the process or you'll end up taking shortcuts that will harm your brand and your business in the long run.

CHAPTER 3

START BEING VISIBLE ...WITH YOUR PROFILE

ARE YOU THE SORT OF PERSON** that likes to bring friends home to your house?

I'll be honest, I never used to be that sort of person growing up. I love my parents, but their idea of interior decorating was cramming every room full of books, suitcases and other items that belonged more in a dump than a house.

I didn't bring friends home because quite frankly I was embarrassed by my house. And when my friends did visit, they usually didn't come back again in a rush because our house didn't have that welcoming feel to it. It wasn't warm and inviting – it was cold (literally) and crowded.

I don't know what kind of house you lived in growing up, or where you live now, but can I put it to you that your LinkedIn profile page is a little like your house?

Sure, you can go out and have a good time on LinkedIn posting content and engaging with other people posts, but having a good house to bring them back to after all that networking is foundational to your LinkedIn success.

Take a moment to ask yourself, "Does my house – my profile page – accurately reflect who I am and what I have to offer as a service? Does it speak directly to my target audience?"

If your answer is no, then it's time for some interior decorating – and that's what this chapter is all about.

THE BAD NEWS ABOUT GOOD PROFILES

Having a good profile page is the starting place for being visible on LinkedIn and standing out from the crowd.

The bad news is that the vast majority of profiles on LinkedIn are *not* good. The good news for you is that if you follow the advice in this chapter of the book, you will move away from the vast majority and into the small minority of people with excellent profiles – and this will truly make you visible in all the right ways.

Another great benefit to having a good LinkedIn profile is that LinkedIn ranks fairly highly in Google, usually within the top three hits in a search. In other words, when people type your name (or your business name) in a Google search, your LinkedIn profile is one of the first things that will come up, so it's vital that what's on your profile accurately reflects your brand and promotes your business.

THE STARTING PLACE: KNOW YOUR AUDIENCE

Finding your target audience is one of the four pillars of LinkedIn success, and we will cover this in great detail in Chapter 6, but when it comes to writing a knockout profile on LinkedIn, the starting place is to *know* your audience.

As a business owner you will (or at least, should!) already have a good idea of who your audience is as these are the people you serve with your products or services.

In my line of work as a LinkedIn Visibility Coach for women entrepreneurs, one question I get fairly often from business owners is, "How do I talk to multiple audiences on LinkedIn?"

The short answer is that you don't.

If you truly want to use LinkedIn as a platform to find, connect with and add value to your target audience and ideal clients, you need to get super-specific about who these people are and narrow down your niche as much as possible.

My business coach puts it like this: "You must alienate in order to resonate."

Even if your business *can* help multiple groups of people at the same time, your marketing efforts and messaging certainly can't reach them all or connect with them all at the same time, so you must decide who to alienate and who to resonate with on LinkedIn. The first place to make that distinction is with your profile.

THE NUTS AND BOLTS OF A GOOD PROFILE

At a basic level, you can measure the strength of your current LinkedIn profile by viewing your profile strength meter via your profile page. This is a bar that appears at the top of your profile with measures ranging from beginner to All-Star, depending on how much of your profile you've completed.

This bar is what LinkedIn uses to prompt you to complete all the relevant sections of your profile. Once you've done this and the meter is full, LinkedIn will award you the "All-Star" prize rating for your efforts, which is what you want to aim for.

An All-Star LinkedIn profile has the following components:

- A good profile photo

- A background photo (banner image)

- A strong headline

- A completed About section

- An up to date Experience section

- An up to date Education section

- Featured skills and endorsements

- Recommendations

- Interests

You can also (and should) add extras such as media samples to the summary and work sections of your profile, and featured content as highlights on your page.

The featured content is a relatively new addition to the LinkedIn profile that allows you to showcase top content you'd like to draw attention to – whether that's an image, video or article promoting your business, or a particularly successful post you've created that you want to draw attention to.

At the time of writing, you can find this section near the top of your profile, just under your About section.

GETTING THINGS RIGHT

We're not going to discuss the work, education or interests section in much detail here. All that's important to note with these areas is that you should complete them with as much detail as necessary.

If you're in business, you won't be using your LinkedIn profile to apply for jobs anyway, so you don't want to waste too much time going into unnecessary detail about your previous jobs. Two or three sentences summarising each role should be fine, unless they're directly relevant to what you do today, in which case you can elaborate further.

Concentrate your efforts instead on writing about your current business and in completing your About section in the best way possible.

YOUR PROFILE PICTURE

There are three areas that immediately capture your attention on anyone's LinkedIn profile – the headline, banner image and profile picture.

Your profile picture is a key element of your brand and for this reason is, arguably, the most critical of these three. LinkedIn users with profile pictures get far more views than those who don't have one.

Your picture is your first chance to make a good impression on your potential clients and others you will meet via the LinkedIn platform.

A good picture should make you look professional but approachable. It should look like you and how you look *today*, not 10 years ago! You want people to be able to recognise you in real life (or virtually) if you were ever to meet, which helps to maintain your credibility.

I change my profile picture on LinkedIn (and everywhere else) roughly every three years to refresh my brand. The last photo I had, however, lasted less than a year before I got rid of it. In this picture, I wasn't the smiley approachable down to earth Mildred that you see on the cover of this book. I was wearing a formal suit – something I rarely do – and, in my

27

view, looking a little stuffy and overly buttoned-up, which didn't feel like me at all. I knew a re-shoot was necessary.

When it comes to getting a good picture for your brand image, working with a skilled professional photographer you trust and feel comfortable with is helpful, as is picking an environment that feels comfortable to you.

I wanted a relaxed casual look for my new photo, so I knew a studio shot wasn't going to cut it. I needed a setting I felt comfortable in and a photographer I could be myself around (I'm not a fan of photoshoots in general, I find them exhausting!) so there were only two choices.

The picture was taken by my brother, a professional photographer and videographer (check him out at vicassovisuals. co.uk or look him up on LinkedIn – Victor Amadiegwu), and the setting was my home. The result? A brand image I absolutely love that totally represents who I am – and one that I get compliments about daily!

Not bad for half a day's work!

The best profile pictures are ones where your face takes up at least 60% of the frame – a close-up shot – and where you're looking directly into the camera. This helps to build trust between you and your viewer from the get-go.

Avoid wearing distracting clothes or jewellery in your picture (unless that's part of your brand). Also avoid pictures with other people or things in the background and uploading poor quality pictures. Selfies (pictures you take of yourself with your phone camera) are not that great either as selfie poses can be restricted and often come across unnatural.

You don't have to use a professional photographer to do your profile picture but the results are usually better when you do – and it's a relatively small investment for something that you can carry with you for years and use across all your on-line platforms.

Being visible is about getting people to know you, like you and trust you. A good profile picture is a great starting place for this to take place. It's the first stop in establishing and promoting your personal brand and making yourself attrac-tive to your ideal clients.

A BACKGROUND PHOTO (BANNER IMAGE)

If you want to stand out and be visible on LinkedIn, having a personalised background photo is a must. So many LinkedIn users miss out on the opportunity this piece of virtual real estate gives you to advertise your brand by keeping the de-fault LinkedIn background or simply uploading a generic picture of a holiday destination they've enjoyed or wish to travel to. This is a major waste.

Consider the banner space on LinkedIn as your personal billboard to promote whatever it is you want people to know about you and your business from the get-go. It should have information about your business (but not too much text), needs to be visually-led and include some form of call to action — whether that's asking people to follow you, connect, schedule a call, visit your website, or something else.

You can design your banner yourself in photoshop, if you know your way around this, use a free template from canva.com, or you can pay a minimal amount to a designer on somewhere like fiverr.com and get yourself a hassle-free bespoke version (which also eliminates the chances of someone else having the same banner template as you).

Your banner doesn't have to stay the same throughout your LinkedIn use — you can (and probably should) change this every so often depending on what you're focusing on in your business for that particular season (for example, while I was writing this book, I changed my banner to one that spoke about my upcoming book and invited people to connect with me for more info), or as your business grows and your brand evolves.

Once you have a good banner installed, what you now have is a billboard that's promoting your brand and advertising your business to potential clients around the clock.

A STRONG HEADLINE

Now that you have your profile and banner sorted, you now need to make sure that the third piece of your dynamic first impressions trio doesn't let the team down.

Your headline appears next to your name in search results, whether someone is connected to you or not, so it is *immediately* visible even before someone lands on your profile.

(Side note: you can hide your profile picture and banner from people you're not yet connected to in the settings section, but you can't hide your headline. I personally don't see the point in hiding either of these things if you're plan on using LinkedIn to get visible so you can promote your brand and attract your ideal clients, so it's not something I would recommend doing.)

You need a strong headline that immediately captures attention, positions you as a credible expert, appeals to your ideal clients and entices them to click your profile to find out more about you – that's a lot to ask for just 120 characters of text (the maximum allowance at the time of writing) but it's entirely doable. Plus, if you really struggle to fit it all in, a little trick you can implement is to write your headline through your phone – it gives you double the amount of characters!

A good headline is specific, written with your target audience in mind and in a style and vocabulary they understand. It's also clear and concise and, for bonus points, memorable.

Treat your headline like a mini mission statement, an elevator pitch if you like, that captures who you are and why people should connect with you. It needs to instantly tell people how you help them, so they are in no doubt of your service provision, and it should speak more about the results you achieve and less about you and your qualifications. You should also aim to incorporate one or two keywords people might use to find your services.

A popular format that you'll find a lot of business people using on LinkedIn is the "I help XXX to do XXX..." Here are a few examples of this:

"I help Entrepreneurs and Leaders tell unforgettable stories and give profitable presentations"

"I help headteachers and other professionals become executive coaches, maximise their impact and empower their teams"

"I help parents raise successful children"

"I help leaders lead so teams can thrive"

Feel free to use this format as a starting place, if it's helpful, but if you really want to stand out and avoid what's becoming a little bit of a cliché on LinkedIn, lose the "I help" and get straight into what you do.

Here's an example from my own current headline:

❋ LinkedIn Visibility Coach for service-based women entrepreneurs ❋ LinkedIn profile writer ❋ #ExJournalist #Author #Speaker #Blogger ➜ DM FOR A CONSULTATION

I used colourful emojis to make my headline stand out and to make it easier for the reader to absorb the information I'm sharing. Feel free to experiment with emojis and symbols in your own headline, providing you keep it professional and true to your brand.

Here are some other good examples that deviate from the "I help" format:

"Social Media Trainer & Personal Branding Cheerleader. Social media strategy, content creation and personal branding to ensure your business shines amongst the competition. Former teacher."

"Communications & Career Specialist | Coaching profession-als & businesses to create compelling content to monetize their brand."

"Chief Executive Officer | Speaker | Storyteller | 20yrs exp run-ning an award-winning Fashion/Lifestyle brand. I am a story-teller by nature. Love to help startups – board level to reach their true potential."

Feel free to use whatever headline format works for you and resonates with your brand. You can always start with some-thing and tweak or change it as you go along. I tweaked and changed my own headline many times before I finally landed on what I have now. Chances are I'll be tweaking it again at some point as my business continues to grow and my brand continues to evolve. Feel free to do the same with yours.

YOUR ABOUT SECTION

Next to your headline, your About section is the most impor-tant piece of text you have on your LinkedIn profile. This is a make or break section. Get this right and you'll have your ideal clients flocking to you to want to work with you (in time); get it wrong and you waste a vital opportunity to sell yourself.

The goal is to find an interesting and genuine way to give an overview of your professional life and describe your current work in a way that appeals to your target audience and also has you come across as a subject matter expert.

Even though the About section is supposed to be about you, technically, I hate to break it to you, but your audience don't actually care about you that much. They care more about themselves and what you can do for them, so if you want to get this part right, the first thing to do is to lose the 'I' focus from your summary and make it about your target audience instead.

Your ideal client needs to read what you write here and feel that you understand them; that you understand the problems they're facing and that you're the person to provide the solution they need. Having less "I" and more "you" in your write-up helps with this.

An effective about section needs to have the following elements:

- An engaging opening

  Start with an opening that appeals directly to your target audience. This could be a short story about something relevant that you or a client of yours experienced, a series of questions, or a direct statement. The idea is to grab your reader's interest immediately so they can read on to the next paragraph, and the one after that and the one after that, and so on... The goal of good copywriting is to engage you with each sentence so you continue reading until you get to the end.

- A solid middle

The middle is where you talk about your mission, the results you achieve for clients, your industry expertise and supporting skills, any relevant personal details, facts and figures that back up your expertise (e.g. how many clients you've helped to achieve the results you deliver), and what the experience of working with you will be like.

- A closing call to action

What do you want your audience to do after reading your profile summary? Do you want them to book a call with you? Buy your book? Join your mailing list...? Whatever it is, take out the guesswork by telling them directly with a clear call to action.

If your call to action is for them to visit your website however, just make sure the URL actually works – you'll be surprised at how many people are driving away potential clients by marketing dead website links!

You want to connect emotionally with your target audience so it's really important that you understand what their pain points are and address these in your summary.

ADDITIONAL QUICK TIPS:

- Write how you speak for a personal touch

- Make it skimmable by spacing out the text

- Include some symbols (emojis) for visual variety – but don't go overboard with this!

- Include some industry-related keywords, where appropriate, to help you get found in searches

- Check and double-check spelling and grammar – there's nothing worse than a good profile with some bad spelling and grammatical errors

Remember, you're working with a maximum of 2,000 characters for this section (around 400 words, give or take) so keep this clear, concise and relevant.

A well-written profile significantly reduces the need for hard selling – in fact, I will go as far as to say it eliminates it altogether since it does the work for you 24/7. Your ideal clients will approach you since it's so clear from your profile that you understand them, know their problems, and have solutions to offer.

I had a client get her first client literally within two days of us working together to transform her profile. The new client told her that she read her profile, loved every word of it and felt that it spoke directly to who she was and where she was at that stage in her life and business. Such is the power of a great profile!

A NOTE ON PROFILE OPTIMISATION

I'll be honest – I actually don't like the word 'optimisation' as it's one of those words that's been so over-used it's become somewhat of a cliché.

But if you really want to make the most of your LinkedIn profile, you really do have to optimise and that means writing your profile in a way that makes you visible in search results relating to your area of business.

So, for example, if you're a "Wellness Coach", you need to be thinking about having that phrase pop up several times on your profile – in the headline and within the about section.

Some people overdo it and cram their entire profile with keywords which may make the LinkedIn algorithm happy, but puts off every other normal human being that reads it. You don't want to do this. What you want to do is choose a few keywords or phrases that you want to be known for and that relate to your business and use this consistently through your marketing. The more niche within the broad industry, the better.

As an example, the micro niche I've chosen for myself is "LinkedIn Visibility Coach". If you search for the title "Coach" on LinkedIn, you will be absolutely inundated with millions of profiles. If you search for "LinkedIn Coach", you will get a lot less but still a sizeable number. If you search for "LinkedIn Visibility Coach", well you may end up with just me! And that's a good thing.

Obviously most people who need a LinkedIn Visibility Coach don't know that's what they need so they don't know that's what they're looking for and won't necessarily type that into the search, but I do come up on searches about LinkedIn experts (LinkedIn periodically alerts you to the search results you're showing up in) and within these, I stand out because of my micro-niche.

> Your niche title will help you enormously in your quest to be visible and stand out in your particular field.

SKILLS & ENDORSEMENTS

LinkedIn gives you the option to add a list of skills to your profile as a way of showcasing your abilities, at a glance, to help people understand your strengths and, ideally, match you with the right opportunities.

You can add any skill you want to your profile – up to a maximum of 50 – but to ensure some kind of quality control, LinkedIn also has the endorsement feature attached to the skills.

This means that people you're directly connected with (your 1st-degree connections) can endorse you for the skills you list, essentially validating that you are indeed good at those skills.

Initially you had to ask your connections to endorse your skills but in recent years LinkedIn has made this an automated process whereby every now and then your connections are prompted to endorse you for a particular skill. They have the option to decline, but if they do endorse you, you will receive a notification alerting you to this.

Your connections can also endorse you for skills you don't want to acknowledge on your profile, maybe because you no longer focus on that side of your work. When this happens, you can simply hide the endorsement.

The skills section act like keywords for your profile that people can use to find you so make sure these are relevant to what you do. The good thing is you can re-order the order by which your skills are displayed on your profile and, at the time of writing, LinkedIn allows you to pin three skills to the top of your skills section to give them an additional boost.

Using this feature and adding and removing skills, as necessary, is a great way to maintain control over this section of your profile and ensure that your most relevant skills are the most visible.

Even though the Skills & Endorsements are useful to have on your profile, people generally don't pay as much attention to them as they do to recommendations so this is where you really want to be spending your time, energy and connection currency.

RECOMMENDATIONS

LinkedIn recommendations are so essential for a well-rounded profile, but yet so neglected by so many people on LinkedIn!

A recommendation is a written statement from a connection that commends you for something. For business purposes, this is where you gather evidence for the success of your work by including client testimonials.

Recommendations displayed on your profile can be read by people who view your profile to see what others have to say about your work.

You can – and should – be regularly requesting recommendations from clients (usually at the completion of the work), customers, colleagues, business partners, peers and pretty much any and everyone you've worked with in some capacity who can vouch for your expertise and/or character. If you're a speaker and you speak at an event, you should request recommendations from the event organisers as well as some of the attendees.

Apart from the personal validation they give you that you're doing great work, recommendations are a brilliant - and essential - way to market your personal brand on LinkedIn.

Every recommendation you receive serves as an endorsement of your personal brand.

They provide credibility about your work, social proof that others are working with you and enjoying the experience, and builds trust with your future clients that you are worth the time and financial investment they need to make to work with you.

You can request recommendations relatively easily by clicking the "ask to be recommended" option on the recommendations part of your profile.

Don't request recommendations from people you haven't worked with and don't agree to do them either for other people.

Once you have some recommendations under your belt, be sure to publicise these on a fairly regularly basis as part of your content strategy (we'll get to that in the next chapter).

FINAL POINTS

You can further enhance your profile – for that All-Star status – by completing additional sections and including details around your accomplishments, volunteer experience and certifications, which LinkedIn says can also increase the amount of times people view your profile – thus boosting your visibility.

A NOTE ON LINKEDIN COMPANY PAGES

As a business owner, it's worth creating a company page for your business but really only for the purpose of giving it additional credibility and also because when you do, and you link it to your profile via the experience section, you now get your company logo appearing next to your job description instead of the bland default grey box.

Posts on company pages, however, generally receive very little to no engagement so don't waste your time trying to build up a following here. You can post on your company page now and again, but it's far better to concentrate your efforts on posting and building engagement on your own personal profile as the "face" behind your company.

This also applies if you have employees. Get them to use their personal profiles to build engagement with your company, as opposed to using the company page. People generally prefer to deal with people, not faceless companies.

CHAPTER 4

START BEING VISIBLE ...WITH YOUR CONTENT

CONTENT IS WITHOUT A DOUBT, CRUCIAL to your LinkedIn success, but also one of the areas people struggle with the most.

If you're not posting content on LinkedIn, you are invisible.

I've seen so many people set up their LinkedIn profile, leave their account to gather dust and then wonder why the platform is not working for them.

For LinkedIn to work for you, *you* have got to work it, and one key way for you to do this is by creating content.

Content is one of the best ways to drive inbound leads to your business. Content employs the method of social selling, where your target market gets to know who you are, like who you are and trust who you are so they can buy from you.

Content marketing – using content as a way of marketing – is essential if you want to promote your brand and attract your ideal clients through LinkedIn. With content marketing, you forego hardcore aggressive sales techniques and opt instead for nurturing, adding value to and building trust with your target audience by providing useful relevant content on a regular basis.

Content marketing allows you to stay in the forefront of your audience's minds – it keeps you visible. Most people need to see you at least 15-20 times before they build enough trust to engage with your services. Content marketing allows this to happen organically and deeply.

It's a long-term strategy but one that works very well and, when done correctly, gives you a consistent flow of people sending messages to your LinkedIn inbox wanting to engage your services.

GOOD CONTENT, BAD CONTENT

Good content on LinkedIn is not copying and pasting your latest blog post URL into your page; it's not incessantly sharing news articles from other sources, and neither is it posting endless daily motivational quote memes from famous thinkers, as you might do on other social media platforms.

In the same vein, regularly sharing content about your hobbies, what you ate that day, or pictures of the latest pet addition to your home might be cute but won't do much for your brand or your business. There is a place for personal content though, and we'll get to that shortly, but for now, we'll define good content as content that is helpful, relevant to your audience and helps them reach their own goals in business or life.

People are looking for good content on LinkedIn – content that inspires, educates, informs and, occasionally, entertains them. They want to learn how to improve their lives and their businesses and LinkedIn provides a great platform to do just that.

When you regularly share content that's helpful and adds value, you start to build trust with your target audience and you create the *pull* marketing effect where *they* approach *you* to ask how they can work with you, not the other way round where you're *pushing* your products and services onto uninterested people.

CONTENT FORMS ON LINKEDIN

Content on LinkedIn can take the form of short-form daily posts on your profile or longer-form articles that stay visible on your page for much longer.

Short form posts can take the form of written content, image posts, video posts, document posts or polls. You can use short-form posts to start conversations around topics relevant to your field, including industry news, trending topics and major events.

Longer form content, like articles, are best for sharing your expertise in more detail. You can use these to really add value to your target audience by going into great detail about a particular topic and offering solutions to their problems, as appropriate.

Some content formats naturally do better than others due to the way the LinkedIn algorithm works in line with what mode of content LinkedIn wants to particularly promote at the time. There was a time when articles were given high priority by the algorithm, which meant that they would reach far more people than a regular post would. This is no longer the case now (though it may well be so once again in future – who knows the mind of LinkedIn!).

At the time of writing, LinkedIn are currently prioritising document posts and video posts. LinkedIn wants to encourage more people to use these features (documents more so) therefore those that do, are rewarded with more visibility – i.e. the LinkedIn algorithm distributes your content to more users so these tend to perform better than regular text or image posts.

You can also share other people's content on your own LinkedIn posts, but this won't drive anywhere as much engagement as creating your own original content. Plus, you'll miss out on a valuable opportunity to position yourself as an expert and build the "know me, like me, trust me" factor with your target audience.

Sharing links to your blog or to articles that lead people away from LinkedIn also doesn't get much traction. Firstly because people tend to like all their content delivered to them straightaway in a single post, without the additional burden of clicking an extra link; and secondly because LinkedIn prioritises content that is directly published in its platform so, at the time of writing, the LinkedIn algorithm penalises posts with external links with less visibility.

DON'T GET STUCK IN A RUT

It's important to vary the type of content you put out on LinkedIn, not just because of the algorithm (I don't advocate over-focusing on the algorithm by the way because they change constantly) but because people have different preferences when it comes to consuming content.

Some of your target audience will prefer the written content you put out, others video, some image-based content, others long-form articles. If you vary your content format regularly, you will be able to cater to the needs of all members of your target audience.

It'll take some trial and error to see what resonates with your audience but once you find what works, you can give them more of the same. But be careful not to get stuck in a rut so that your content becomes 'samey'. Every now and again break up your regular schedule of content with personal content that isn't wholly business related to give your audience an insight into who you are. This is where the 80/20 theme rule comes into it (we'll get to this shortly).

Sharing helpful content helps to establish your expertise and credibility and builds trust with your audience; sharing appropriate personal content, in a way that's authentic to you, cements likeability and loyalty within your target audience.

When you take the time to create content that adds value to your target audience, you immediately start to rise above the crowd. You're on your journey to becoming visible and being seen, heard and remembered for all the right reasons.

CREATING CONTENT

Sharing content regularly on LinkedIn allows you to position yourself as a credible expert, demonstrate thought leadership in your field, and connect with your target audience.

There are many approaches to creating content for LinkedIn. You can go by themes, days of the week, type of content, and much more.

But the starting place for all of it (and for most things LinkedIn), is to have your target audience in mind. The more in-depth knowledge you have about your audience, the better you will be able to create a content strategy that caters to their needs.

Here are some questions to ask yourself to gain some clarity around this:

- Who is your target audience?

- What are they interested in?

- What are their pain points? What problems or challenges are they facing right now?

- What are their aspirations?

- What solutions does your business offer for these challenges or in support of these aspirations?

Once you have clarity on your audience and the type of content that can best serve them, based on your area of expertise, the next step is to create a content plan.

The best way to create content that adds value is to teach your audience to do for themselves what they could pay you to do for them! It sounds counter-intuitive, I know, but freely sharing helpful and valuable content with your target audience not only demonstrates your seemingly unlimited knowledge and expertise in your field, it also builds trust with your audience and actually makes them more willing to pay you – and to pay you more – for your services. It's the psychological thought process of, "If her free stuff is *this* good, then her paid stuff must be even more phenomenal!"

CONTENT PLANNING

Generating content on a consistent basis is by far one of the hardest things to do on LinkedIn, but it doesn't have to be.

Good content on LinkedIn requires strategic planning and execution.

If you want to be successful on LinkedIn, you must plan your content. It's vital that you have a strategy and that you set out regular time each week to plan, write and execute.

This will be the difference between waking up each day trying to think of something to post – and failing to post because nothing came – and waking up prepared and knowing what you're posting ahead of time so you can spend the rest of your allocated LinkedIn time engaging with your network.

If you struggle with putting out content, a simple strategy that will help is to have an overall theme that you want to be known and remembered for by your audience. This theme should be directly related to your line of work, if you intend to use LinkedIn to build your brand and your business, and it should relate to the issues your target audience face on a daily basis.

You can have one massive overall theme that you talk about on a regular basis, or you can have several smaller themes within the big theme that you focus on specifically.

So, if for example the big theme is entrepreneurship, smaller themes within that could be solo entrepreneurship, marketing for small businesses, personal branding, etc. The more you niche down, the better. A tighter niche allows you to come up with content more easily and helps you to be better remembered by your target audience.

Theming your content will help you plan in advance, bypass writers block (most of the time), and connect with your audience effectively. And, of course, it keeps you visible by helping you show up every day on LinkedIn so you're first in mind when your audience needs you.

Choose a theme that excites you within your field of expertise and that relate to your target audience. When you do this, and you couple it with regular activities where you listen to your target audience (through engagement on your posts, for example, or sales calls), you will find it easier to keep content ideas flowing week after week.

Sometimes you may get spontaneous content ideas that are timely (for example, a response to something that's happened in the news or a new and relevant development in your business or personal life) but deviate from your theme for that day, week or month, when that happens, go with it – as long as it still aligns with your brand values – as sometimes these produce the best engagement with your audience.

I generally plan my content a month in advance, with an overall theme (my big theme is LinkedIn and within that are several smaller themes such as profile, content, engagement, audience etc). The actual day-to-day content for each week, I plan and write up a week in advance, and then do final preps and edits on the content the night before I'm scheduled to post.

When you have a plan in place for your content, you will find it much easier to come up with ideas and, more importantly, to plan ahead so you're never stuck on what to post on a particular day.

A NOTE ON REPURPOSING CONTENT

When you create content, particularly a longer piece of content like an article for LinkedIn, your blog or your newsletter mailing list, think about how you can re-use some or all of that content in a different context or in a fresh new way.

This is called repurposing content. Repurposing content is when you modify content you've created for one avenue and re-publish it somewhere else in a different context.

So, for example, a 5-minute how-to video you've created on a particular topic relating to your business can be dissected into bite-sized text pieces for your daily LinkedIn posts; an excerpt from an article you've written can be captured as a quote, attached to an image, and turned into a graphic post; an audio you've created on your podcast can easily translate into an article, a video excerpt (with a still image) and more.

Repurposing content is not only easier and less time-consuming than creating new and original content all the time, it also gives you maximum visibility for that particular piece of content, which is always a good thing.

THE 80/20 THEME RULE

When it comes to deciding how much of a particular type of content you should put out on LinkedIn, it's important to remember that a key component of being visible is to build the "know me, like me, trust me" factor we spoke about in earlier chapters.

A good guideline is to split your content using the 80/20 ratio: 80% of your content should have a business-focused, value-adding angle to it; the other 20% should be reserved for personal posts that give an insight into your life, hobbies, issues you care about, or anything else that isn't directly business related.

For example, I use my 20% to talk about books I'm currently reading, films I've watched, current affairs that have captured my interest, fitness challenges I've taken part in, and so on. I've seen others share posts about their weekend baking habits, teaching their kid to ride a bike, videos of their favourite TED talks, and much more.

(Side note: most of these types of personal posts tend to appear on the weekends and generally seem to be better received then too. Posting on weekends is perfectly normal on LinkedIn. I generally don't do it unless it's one of these personal type posts or unless I have something I really want to say that can't wait until Monday. It's totally up to you to decide whether you want to show up on LinkedIn at the weekends or not.)

You can also use the 80/20 theme rule as a guideline for how much of your day-to-day content should be promotional. In order to build trust and credibility with your audience, 80% of your content should be focused on purely adding value. The other 20% can be promotional. These are the posts where you're giving a specific call to action around your business – whether that's buy a book, join a webinar, schedule a call, book a service and so on. This is roughly the equivalent of one post a week.

But even when you do these kinds of posts, you don't have to make them "salesy" – they can still offer value to your audience but with a specific call to action that directly translates to business results for you.

I've done posts like this where I've talked about the importance of having a good LinkedIn profile, for example, and then at the end of the post asked people to contact me to book a strategy call to discuss their LinkedIn profile.

If you want to successfully use LinkedIn to promote your brand and attract your ideal clients, you'll want to keep it at the forefront of your mind that the aim of your content (and everything else you do on LinkedIn) is to build relationships, not to sell. Content that aggressively sells is a major turn-off for most people.

Establishing and nurturing relationships with your target audience will eventually lead to sales because people buy from people that they know, like and trust – especially in service-based businesses.

Your content should always add value to your audience, provide ongoing solutions to their problems and deliver answers to their questions.

Don't worry about giving too much knowledge away for free – I fully subscribe to the belief that the more you give, the more you get in return, and that can manifest as more business ideas, more income, or new opportunities that previously weren't on your radar. Also, the more value you give through your content, the more trust you will build in your audience that you are someone with their best interests at heart, not someone who just wants their money.

Once you deliver value through your content and you do this well enough and consistently enough for long enough, you will start to find that your sales conversations will be initiated by your connections, not the other way round. Your ideal clients will send *you* messages in your inbox asking how they can work with you and, for the most part, because you've demonstrated so much value already and they now trust you, they are usually ready and willing to pay your prices without hesitation.

AIM TO START A CONVERSATION

The aim of every post you put out on LinkedIn should be to start or continue a conversation.

Truly understanding this is a game-changer for your content production as it changes the focus from counting likes and comments to 'what did I learn today from other people?' or 'what did I make people think differently about today?'

If the aim of the post is to start a conversation, then the post itself should make it easy for people to join in the conversation and the quickest and best way to do this is to ask a question at the end and invite your audience to share their thoughts in the comments section. We'll talk about this some more in the next chapter on engagement.

HOW TO STRUCTURE YOUR POSTS FOR EASY ENGAGEMENT

The way you structure your posts also helps or hinders engagement. LinkedIn allows you 2,500 characters per post. You can use as much or as little of this when you post.

If you are writing longer form text-only content where you plan to use all the word count, make this as easy to read as possible by keeping your sentences short, spacing out your paragraphs, including visuals (such as emojis) and using as few words as necessary. Aim to be brief and of course include a call to action.

Structuring your posts like this make it easier for people to want to engage when they're scrolling through a noisy LinkedIn feed, and if the content is also good alongside your structure, you're winning all the way!

BONUS CONTENT WRITING TIPS

- Think like a journalist: to really up your content game, include catchy headlines, snappy intros and clear points in your post.

- Keep it concise: If you can say it in one word, don't use two.

- Always include a clear call to action: this could be a question for engagement or a business-focused directive, such as join your mailing list.

- Include visuals: this could either emojis, gifs or pictures that are relevant to your post.

- Use videos for added visibility boost: make sure these are native videos (videos directly uploaded into Linked-In) and not links to YouTube or other video sites. Native videos perform a whole lot better than video links because LinkedIn don't want you driving their users away to other platforms, as we already discussed. Shorter videos also tend to work better than longer ones.

- Add captions to your videos: this is helpful for people who are viewing your video in a setting (such as work) where they are unable to turn the sound on. It's also helpful for those with hearing impairments.

SETTING CONTENT GOALS

You need a goal driven content marketing strategy – i.e there must be a point to it.

Like all your other business marketing activities, it's important that you set tangible goals around your LinkedIn activities so you can measure your impact and progress and tweak accordingly, where necessary.

These could be goals around how many connections / followers you have in a certain month, how many prospective clients reach out to you via inbox, how many people join your mailing list as a result of your activities, and so on. You're not looking for vanity metrics here – like how many reactions you get on an individual post – unless it has a direct impact on your business.

I've seen people on LinkedIn whose sole job seems to be to spark daily discussions or debates about random controversial subjects. Even though these kind of posts generally get good engagement, by way of comments, I often question whether it translates into actual business results, and if you're on LinkedIn to promote your brand and attract your ideal clients, what you need is business results, not quick wins with going viral.

You can certainly explore issues that are relevant to your industry, even if they might be controversial. With these, you need to state your position and stand by it. I once did a post on whether it was okay to like your own posts on LinkedIn, and I stood firmly on the no side. The post erupted into a wild debate with over 200 comments (which is a lot for the audience I had at the time) and people offering views from both sides of the fence. This post gained me a lot of new followers, which was relevant because it's a topic that I speak about anyway.

There's nothing wrong with posting a controversial debate-worthy post now and again, if it fits in with your style, your audience and your topics, but if doing so doesn't help you reach whatever business goals you've pre-determined for yourself, you're wasting precious time.

The same goes for the kind of content you engage with on LinkedIn, but we'll get to that in the next chapter.

SOME CONTENT NEED TO KNOWS

There are a few things you'll come across as you embark on your content creation journey on LinkedIn. I've listed some of the important ones below and how they relate to you.

HASHTAGS

It's important to use hashtags in your posts as a way of indicating what the post is about, at a glance, but also for added visibility. Hashtags are searchable and can be found and followed by people interested in those particular themes or topics, so using relevant hashtags in your post potentially allows your content to be discovered by LinkedIn members outside of your existing network.

When you write a post, you can use the hashtags LinkedIn recommends at the bottom of your post editing window, or you can choose your own hashtags based on your general content themes (as long as it's relevant).

You can also create a hashtag to monitor a particular series of conversation you want to have on LinkedIn (for example, some people create a hashtag around their name so their audience can use it to keep track of their posts on a particular topic. When I used to blog more regularly, I would add the hashtag #mildredwrites to posts that referenced my blog of the same name).

Find a few hashtags you want to be known for, that relate to your business, and use them as regularly as possible.

#TRENDING POSTS

You can trend on LinkedIn, maybe a little easier than on other platforms, but it all comes down to posting a great piece of content. Sometimes this can be picked up by LinkedIn's algorithm under the hashtag you've used and it can start trending which means people not connected to you can see it. When this happens, you'll usually get a notification from LinkedIn telling you that you're trending.

You may find that you get a notification telling you that you're trending on a particular topic (based on the hashtag you assigned to your post) but you have little engagement on that particular post by way of likes and comments. In cases like this, it's nothing to get too excited about unfortunately, as it's just LinkedIn's way of giving you a pat on the back for creating content in order to encourage you to continue.

DON'T POST TOO MUCH

How much is too much posting? Answer – it depends.

LinkedIn posts have a long shelf life and you can get people liking or commenting on your posts many days after you've posted and each time that happens, and you respond to it, it reignites the conversation.

Articles have an even longer shelf life as they're easier to find. I still get people to this day like and comment on articles I shared years back on topics I no longer speak about today (side note: if you have old articles that are no longer reflective of your current brand or business, you can choose to remove them from LinkedIn or keep them there for additional credibility, if they're not damaging to your current brand).

Posting too much reduces the engagement potential for your posts. Posting once a day is ideal as it allows enough time for engagement but also so that your posts won't compete with each other for attention.

If you really must post twice in the same day, leave several hours between the posts to reduce the engagement clash. Any more than twice a day and you become a spammer – LinkedIn isn't Twitter! (Side note: there are a few major influencers on LinkedIn who break this rule and are still successful. They are the exception and not the rule.)

CONTENT PRACTICES TO AVOID

- Tagging unrelated people in your posts: People do this as a way to increase visibility and boost engagement. This is not only annoying to the people who are being tagged, but if you continually tag people who don't respond to your posts, the LinkedIn algorithm will start to penalise you as it's picking up negative signals that your content isn't actually very good and therefore not worth promoting.

- Using a million and one hashtags: the hashtag vomit look is not appealing on the eye. Most people will skip over your content on their feed for this very reason.

- Direct sales pitch posts which add no value: no one likes to read these kind of posts, not even you, so why do it?

- Posting the same content to multiple places on LinkedIn: People generally tend to do this with blog posts. It's called spamming. This is damaging to your brand and definitely not a good way to win business.

- Sending your connections a direct message to tell them about your posts or articles: Again, unless it's directly relevant to them and of value, don't do this. It's just as bad as tagging, perhaps even more annoying.

Implement the good practices of content creation and avoid the bad ones and you'll be well on your way to mastering the next golden pillar of LinkedIn success – engagement!

CHAPTER 5

START BEING VISIBLE ...WITH YOUR ENGAGEMENT

IF YOU REALLY WANT TO SUCCEED at using LinkedIn to promote your brand and attract your ideal clients, you can't stop at having a good profile and creating good content, you need to go a step further and start being visible with your engagement.

What do I mean by engagement? Essentially, how you relate to the other 700million+ users on LinkedIn (or however many of these are in your own network).

Engagement is important because this is what allows you to build relationships with your target audience, peers and other LinkedIn users. It's where networking truly happens and social selling takes place effortlessly.

As with everything else LinkedIn, you need to be intentional about how you engage so you can maximise the time you invest on the platform and see tangible results from it (in the long run).

To do this, there are three areas of engagement to focus on:

1. Your own content

2. Other people's content

3. Direct message conversations

Before we get into each of these, it's helpful to describe what engagement looks like on LinkedIn and that is simply reacting to a post (with a like, love, support etc), leaving comments on a post or article, sharing content someone else has posted, or having conversations in direct messaging.

When you carry out any one of these activities, you are engaging. When you carry out all of them on a regular basis, you are truly making the most out of LinkedIn and well on your way to using this platform to effectively promote your brand and attract your ideal clients.

ENGAGE WITH YOUR OWN CONTENT

The first place to start your engagement is with your own content.

I don't mean liking or commenting on your own posts (this is a divisive topic on LinkedIn — some say you should like and comment on your own posts for additional visibility, others say it's unnecessary and feels a little desperate. I'll let you make up your own mind!), I mean engaging with the people who engage with you when you put out content.

As you get into the habit of posting useful content on LinkedIn on a regular basis, people will start to engage with you by way of likes, comments and even sharing your content. Acknowledge and validate these people by engaging with them in return on your own posts. Not only is it a polite thing to do, it also makes people feel good and encourages them to keep engaging with you in future.

You don't have to do anything elaborate to acknowledge and validate those who engage with you. Returning the engagement is as simple as liking the comment and replying to anyone who leaves a comment.

It also means thanking those who have shared your content (again, by liking and commenting on the share in their own feed) and I personally go the extra step of reaching out to people who have engaged with my content – whether by likes, comments, or shares – to thank them for the engagement and invite them into my network via a personalised connection request, if they're not already a part of it.

It's important to regularly check your recent posts and sort the comments by "most recent" to make sure you haven't missed engaging with anyone, as LinkedIn notifications can sometimes be faulty. This can be time-consuming but I truly believe if someone's made the effort to take a little bit of time out of their day to engage with our content, the least we can do is take a little bit of time in return to show some gratitude.

I appreciate the time factor really kicks in if you have a particularly viral post with hundreds of engagement, or you regularly get high numbers of engagement on your content. Where that's the case, aim for liking the comments at the very least, but if you go beyond that, people will notice and appreciate you for it.

There's an influencer I follow on LinkedIn and have followed on different social media platforms for several years because of his great business advice and family values that resonate with me. His name is Paul Carrick Brunson and even though he has well over 220,000 followers on LinkedIn (at the time of writing) and gets lots of engagement in his posts, he takes time to respond to comments individually, which I've always appreciated as a receiver. As a result of this demonstration of care and appreciation for his community, Paul has built up a very likeable reputation and a loyal following of people that are always ready to buy his services and support him on any project he gets involved in. His "know me, like me, trust me" currency is very high!

HOW DO YOU GET OTHERS TO ENGAGE WITH YOUR CONTENT?

Now that we have the right protocol in place for returning engagement on your own posts, the question lies, how do you actually get others to engage with you in the first place?

The answer is with a question!

Your LinkedIn audience actually *want* to engage with you, but often they don't know it's okay to do so unless you *explicitly* tell them to. This is where asking a question comes in handy!

Questions invite your audience to engage with you by offering their own opinions on your content – or asking further questions of their own (which is great for you as you can use these to develop future content).

But what kind of question should you be asking?

First, let's look at what not to ask:

- *Lazy* questions that require just a yes or no answer generally don't provoke a need to respond;

- *Essay* questions that require your audience to think long and hard create barriers in engagement;

- *Rhetorical* questions where you've already answered the question leave no need for engagement.

On the plus side, these types of questions work well:

- *Easy* questions that have a low barrier to entry (i.e almost anyone can answer it);

- *Relevant* questions which relate to the content of your post;

- *Genuine* questions that emerge when you actually care about what your audience has to say.

Obviously your content needs to be interesting enough to evoke a response, but if you're struggling to get engagement on your posts, try asking a question and see what kind of response you get.

The first few times you do this might feel uncomfortable, scary even, but don't quit. Continue to ask questions at the end of every post and invite your audience to the conversation.

There will be days when no one responds, or no one likes your posts, or people just generally don't behave in the way you want or expect them to. This is normal and part and parcel of growing. Learn any lessons you need to from it, adjust if necessary, and then get up and go again the next day. Like with everything else LinkedIn, consistency is key. Keep showing up regardless of the results.

A NOTE ON EARLY ENGAGEMENT

Because of the way the LinkedIn algorithm works, early engagement – when people engage with your content as soon as you put it out – helps to determine the overall visibility of your post. The more people engage with your content close to the time of posting, the more it signals to the algorithm that this is a good post worthy of more people seeing it, therefore the further the post is distributed in terms of landing on more people's feeds.

If you want to take advantage of early engagement, be sure to post at a time that a) your target audience are active (recommended posting times for the most engagement tends to be early mornings, mid-week lunchtimes and early evenings), and b) you're available to engage, particularly within the first hour.

ENGAGE WITH OTHER PEOPLE'S CONTENT

As you start putting out your own content on a regular basis, you'll start to notice some of the same names popping up time and time again on your posts, whether to like it, comment on it, or share your content.

What's happening here is that you're starting to build an online community – a tribe, if you like – of people who like and regularly engage with your content. This community will be made up of any combination of your target audience (we'll talk about how to attract them in the next chapter), previous or existing clients, peers, friends, family, colleagues, general supporters, and maybe the odd influencer or thought leader.

It's important to acknowledge and nurture this community by also making time to engage with their own content as much as possible. You can then widen your net and find other people's content, beyond your community, to engage with on a daily basis.

Engaging with other people's content is a great way to build relationships and, on a more selfish note, it raises your visibility by bringing more eyeballs to your own profile. While posting too much is a bad idea, engaging with people via commenting definitely isn't! In fact, you should aim to engage at least five times as much as you post – so if you're posting once a day, you need to be engaging at least five times a day, preferably with five different connections.

And by engagement, I'm not referring to simply liking people's posts here – that is the very basic level of engagement. If you want to rise above that and really use engagement as a way to solidify your relationships, build your credibility in your field, showcase your expertise, give an insight into your personality and raise your visibility, you need to be doing more than liking posts – you need to be leaving actual comments. Not, "I like this", "great post", "thanks for sharing" types of comments, but meaningful comments related to the content and, preferably, to the question the connection has posed on their post.

ENGAGING WITH A DULL OR NOISY FEED

One of the challenges people face when it comes to engaging on LinkedIn is when their feed is too dull or too noisy. Every day is a struggle to find something worth liking, commenting or sharing. Have you ever experienced this? I know I have!

There's no doubt that finding posts to engage with is hard to do when you have an overcrowded feed with lots of people vying for your attention at the same time. Even worse than hard, it can feel overwhelming when you've got limited time and you're scrolling and scrolling through hundreds of dull posts to find something worth commenting on, or at the very least publicly liking.

The good news is there is a solution to this.

The first place to start is by engaging with those who already engage with you, as we previously discussed. Then you want to allocate some time to engaging with content on your feed that actually interests you, as these are the ones that allow you to naturally leave meaningful comments that showcase your expertise, values and/or personality.

To find these types of content, you need to train the LinkedIn algorithm to bring them to your feed.

What you currently see on your news feed is determined by the LinkedIn algorithm, which has two primary goals – to prioritise relevant content and to promote engagement. In other words, it wants to show you content that's relevant to you so that you can engage with the content and in so doing spend more time on the platform.

At the time of writing, the algorithm determines "relevant" content as content from people you actually know (i.e. your first-degree connections) and people you've interacted with directly in some form, whether that's through comments, shares, reactions to their posts, or direct messaging. It also considers other information on your profile, such as your interests and skills (which is why that section is important for you to fill out and keep updated), and who you work with.

The other consideration of relevancy is content that relates to topics you care about, and the algorithm can work this out again based on content you already engage with, groups you're part of, and the hashtags, people, and pages you currently follow.

If you find that your feed isn't bringing you interesting and relevant content to engage with, you can actively train the algorithm to do better. Here are some actions you can take to influence the algorithm:

- Follow influencers and thought leaders in your field and comment on their posts

- Follow and comment on posts by peers in your field

- Follow and comment on posts by active organisations relevant to your field

- Follow and comment on hashtags relevant to your business

- Follow and comment on posts in active groups relevant to your field or target market

- Engage with LinkedIn's recommended content related to your field (such as featured news articles)

- Unfollow anyone's content you don't find interesting (you have this option hidden behind the three dots that's at the top right hand side of every post)

- Use LinkedIn's "hide this post" option to hide boring or irrelevant posts (also hidden under the three dots)

After some time consistently doing these actions, you will start to notice a change in your feed. It will becoming much more interesting and you'll have a much easier time engaging with your network.

STRATEGIC ENGAGEMENT

Engaging with content that interests you is a great place to start with engagement, but if you really want to start being visible to your target audience in order to promote your brand and attract your ideal clients, you need to engage strategically too.

What does this look like practically? It means:

- Getting involved in conversations in the places where your target audience hang out (this could be in groups, around an influencer / thought leader's posts, or on active company pages).

- Taking part in conversations that allow you to showcase your expertise (you can find such conversations in the places mentioned above, but also by searching hashtags, searching "by content" with keywords, and by keeping an eye out on your feed for conversations where you can add value as an expert in your field).

When you engage with other people's content through leaving meaningful comments of your own, you experience the additional benefit of exposing your profile to other people who read that post.

If you are carrying out strategic engagement and you're commenting on things your target audience are interested in, this could potentially produce prospective clients for you either by them engaging with your comment and reaching out to connect with you after viewing your profile, or by you actively reaching out to connect with them, using that content as a basis for your request.

If you're going to do the latter, personalise the connection request with a message that clearly marks how you came across them and why you're reaching out to connect. It doesn't have to be in-depth – it can be something as simple as, *"Thank you for engaging with my comment on XXXXX's post about XXXXX. Would love to connect."*

ENGAGE IN DIRECT MESSAGE CONVERSATIONS

I always follow up new connections with inbox messages to start conversations as a way of engagement. Nothing spammy or promotional, just a friendly personalised, *"Hey XXXXX, thanks for connecting with me. Would love to know what made you reach out and if there's any way I can specifically help you..."* type of message.

If the person is in my target audience, I would have personalised the connection request in the first place so I would now go in with a follow up message to thank them for connecting, comment on one thing they've said on their profile or mentioned in a post, and offer my assistance should they need it. I've found these messages to be great for starting conversations and building relationships, whether for direct business purposes or otherwise.

You can use good old text for these conversations or you can opt for leaving a voice note (maximum allowance of one minute) – an underused tool for LinkedIn messaging which makes a great impression. If you really want to go for the wow factor, and you might want to do this on occasion, you can record and send a personalised video.

Whichever way you choose to engage via your inbox, I don't recommend using automation tools but doing it manually where possible, for the personalised effect. I usually block time out on a daily basis to go through my inbox and start these conversations. Building relationships is a key part of social selling, so it's a time investment worth making.

BONUS ENGAGEMENT OPPORTUNITY – LINKEDIN LIVE

At the time of writing, LinkedIn has started to roll out a new and exciting feature that provides the ultimate engagement opportunity with your audience.

LinkedIn Live allows you to broadcast live on LinkedIn (at the moment through using a third party software system like Streamyard) and interact with your audience – through comments – in real time.

Other platforms have had the ability to do live videos for a while, LinkedIn dragged its feet about it, and even now it's a feature they're restricting so not all users have it. You have to apply for it and they will make a decision as to whether you can have it or not.

I was blessed to have been approached by LinkedIn and given the Live licence. Having used it several times already, I can tell you it's a fantastic new addition to LinkedIn and one that will really help you take your engagement with your audience to new levels once you get it.

FINAL THOUGHTS

It's important to develop a strong network of people who can spread the word about your brand and services. You create this network through a strategic plan (we'll cover this in audience) and you nurture them through engagement.

CHAPTER 6

START BEING VISIBLE ...TO YOUR AUDIENCE

EVERYTHING WE'VE DISCUSSED SO FAR around crafting your profile, content and engagement is important for promoting your brand and attracting your ideal clients through LinkedIn, but if you really want to profit financially from this platform, this last key of being visible to your target audience is crucial.

LinkedIn has some pretty advanced search features that allows you to really narrow down on your target audience based on specific details such as demographics, job function, level of job seniority, education, skills, industry, company name, company size, interests and much more.

This function isn't restricted to just the paid premium account either (I'll touch on LinkedIn premium versus free later) – you can carry out these searches with the free account, but there is an unidentified limit that kicks in when you "abuse" it and become what LinkedIn calls a "power user". When this happens, LinkedIn then limits your search for the rest of month and suggests you upgrade to the paid version of the platform to experience all the benefits of un-restricted search.

If you really want to find and connect with your target audience however, the starting place is not to dive into LinkedIn search, but to first be *crystal clear* about exactly who your target audience is.

An in-depth insight into your target audience makes it easier to write your profile with them in mind, create content that resonates with and adds value to them, and engage strategi-cally with them in a way that translates into real business results.

As a business owner, you should already have a good idea of who your target audience is and be able to translate this into

LinkedIn, but just in case you need more clarification, here are a few questions to ask yourself that will help:

1) What is the core service or offering you provide?

2) Who would most benefit from this?

3) What are their primary pain points?

4) What is your unique selling point as a business or brand?

The more narrow (niched) you are on who you're targeting, the better for you, results-wise.

Once you have the criteria for your target audience, the next step is to find them on LinkedIn and attract and invite them into your network as followers or connections (we'll talk about the difference between these later). The wider your network, the better your prospects are for reaching your target audience.

FINDING YOUR AUDIENCE THROUGH DIRECT SEARCH

If you don't have a LinkedIn premium account, it is still possible to find your target audience on LinkedIn through direct search. This is where you enter specific keywords into LinkedIn's search facility to locate your audience based on your set criteria.

So, for example, I coach women with service-based businesses on how to use LinkedIn to grow their business and their brand. My target audience are women (surprise, surprise!), who have businesses where they deliver a service to people, and have less than 1,000 connections in their network (this is usually indicative of someone who is still learning the ropes around LinkedIn use).

These women are likely to have the titles of founder, coach, consultant, or something along theses lines, in their profile so one of these keywords is what I would enter into the search box primarily before sifting through the people results to find who meets the rest of my criteria (such as location, industry etc).

The key is to find members of your target audience that are *active* on LinkedIn – not ones who have set up accounts at some point and have left it to gather dust. Sending connection requests to ghost accounts doesn't help your business in any way.

To find active accounts, you have to then go into each of the profiles individually and scroll down to their "activity" section. At this point, I would generally check for people who have been active in the last 1-2 weeks, either through posting content of their own or by engaging with other people.

It's also worth scrolling down further into their activities to see if they've regularly been active or whether this recent activity is a one-off. If their activity levels sufficiently meets your criteria, you can then reach out and follow them.

CONNECTIONS VS FOLLOWERS: THE DIFFERENCE

There are two ways you can be part of someone's network on LinkedIn, and they yours – by connecting or by following.

"Connect" is the default button LinkedIn shows users who view your profile. When someone reaches out to connect with you (and you accept), they now become part of your network as a "first-degree connection". This means that you get to see their content in your feed and they get to see yours. It also means that you get to message each other for free (sending messages to people outside of your connections is paid-for feature reserved for premium accounts), and you get to see who they're connected with and they yours. You can have a maximum of 30,000 connections in your network.

When you "follow" someone, on the other hand, or they follow you, they do not become a connection (since you haven't connected) so you have access to see their content but they can't see yours (unless they follow back) and you can't message each other. There are no limits to how many followers you can have on LinkedIn.

It's a good idea to switch your default button from connect to follow, through your privacy settings, once you start creating content and your network grows to a substantial size (I'd recommend of at least 1,000 connections). This switch allows more people to plug in to your content, which in turn raises your visibility, further promotes your brand and increases the potential of attracting your ideal clients.

Switching to followers also has the added benefit of growing your network much faster than having the connect button as it removes the additional fear some people may have of sending a connection request and being rejected.

Unless you have a compelling non-spammy or non-salesy personalised introduction message that your target audience will love (and you can find out by testing some personalised requests and monitoring the response rate based on the messages), I'd recommend following your audience initially instead of connecting with them.

When you follow someone, they get notified of this, which puts your name on their radar. You also now get to see their content on your feed, which presents you with the opportunity to get to know them and engage with them well before entering into any form of sales conversations or making a connection request.

It's important to note, however, that you can't rely on the LinkedIn algorithm alone to bring the content of your target audience to your feed, especially as there's so much other content to contend with, as we've already discussed.

All this searching and saving of profiles is *much* easier when it's done with Sales Navigator – LinkedIn's inbuilt sales system – but if you're not in the position financially or otherwise, to use Sales Navigator, it's a good idea to create your own spreadsheet to monitor and keep track of the people you've identified as potential clients so you can remember to engage with them on a regular basis.

A NOTE ON LINKEDIN PREMIUM SERVICES

LinkedIn is a free platform but like most businesses, they have to make their money somehow and one of the ways they do that is through their premium account products.

There are four types of premium accounts you can sub-scribe to on LinkedIn but the two that relates to business people are Premium Business and Sales Navigator (the other two are Premium Career for advancing your job search, and Recruiter Lite for finding and hiring talent).

Premium Business is useful for getting detailed business insights about your business, but the standout premium product for business owners is Sales Navigator as it has a powerful database that allows you to find and keep track of potential clients.

I don't recommend getting Sales Navigator until you've mastered the basics of LinkedIn (the four pillars of LinkedIn success) on the free account, otherwise you won't get the best use out of it and you'll be wasting your money.

GROWING YOUR NETWORK

There are two main school of thoughts when it comes to growing your network on LinkedIn and two main camps of people – there are those who are super-guarded and there are those with no boundaries at all.

The guarded camp maintain a very tight control over their network. They only let people in that they actually know in real life or have connected with in some way outside of LinkedIn. These people treat connection requests from strangers with suspicion and, more often than not, decline these requests.

The no boundaries camp are at the opposite end of the scale. They want to grow their network and they want to grow it fast, so they reach out to any and everyone and let any and everyone in.

Both approaches have their pros and cons.

The guarded camp tend to maintain a small but engaged network, but miss out on the uniqueness of LinkedIn – building relationships with people that can potentially expand your world and grow your business.

The no boundaries camp build a large network and have interesting variety in that network but the lack of focus can be costly when it comes to driving engagement on their content and actually gaining clients from LinkedIn.

When I first started out on LinkedIn over a decade ago, I was on the guarded side as I wanted to maintain the integrity of my network (and plus LinkedIn used to issue a scary warning message each time you reached out to add someone to your network that was something along the lines of "Do you know this person? Only connect with people you know"!).

Over the years I gradually swung over to the other side and let any and everyone into my network for the price of asking, which diluted the quality of my network.

The best approach is to be somewhere in the middle. Maintain some quality control by vetting the people you allow into your network, but at the same time, be open enough not to be overly strict with this criteria.

This is why I came up with the '60-20-20 principle'.

THE 60-20-20 PRINCIPLE

When it comes to growing your network on LinkedIn, I like to follow a simple formula I call the 60-20-20 principle.

The 60-20-20 principle is a good way to create a healthy and varied network that opens you up to the possibility of attracting your ideal clients but also attracting other opportunities that support your business or your brand.

With the 60-20-20 principle, your network would look something like this:

- 60% target audience

- 20% industry peers

- 20% everyone else

As a business person, the vast amount of your time and energy should be spent bringing in clients therefore 60% of those in your LinkedIn network should be your target audience.

20% should be your peers – people in similar fields to you that you can learn from, refer business to and so on. This can also include people you admire, whether that's influencers in your field or business celebrities and thought leaders.

Having this group in your network and engaging with them helps to establish your credibility and expertise. When you engage meaningfully with your peers, a mutual respect develops and as they start to trust you, they'll start to include you in their conversations, which in turn improves your visibility by exposing their audience to you.

The final 20% of your network can be any and everyone. Anyone who engages with your content by liking, commenting or sharing deserves an invitation to your network. Friends, family, former colleagues, neighbours, should be welcomed into this category too. This group is your fan group, so to speak – people who are likely to support you (by engaging with your content) just because it's you and in so doing raise your visibility and extend your reach on the platform. Additional and sometimes unexpected opportunities tend to come from this group.

The 60-20-20 principle doesn't have to be an exact science. There's no need to whip out your calculator and start crunching numbers to figure out who's in your network, but what it does mean is that as you increase your network and with every connection request you receive or send, ask yourself, "where does this person fit in my 60-20-20?"

Aim to consciously add far more people into your network that are in your target audience than others. This will help to ensure you have an engaged network of people who are *actually* interested in your content and have the potential to engage with your services.

This is crucial as a business owner – you're not on LinkedIn just to make friends, you're on LinkedIn to build a business that meets your financial goals and helps you live the kind of life you want with the people you love.

GROWING YOUR NETWORK ORGANICALLY

Growing your network is essential if you are going to start being visible on LinkedIn. The simple reason for this is that a larger network widens your reach – you become more visible to more people and therefore increase the probability of at-tracting your ideal clients through your activities.

The key here is growing your network organically. That means not using automation tools, or anything like that, and having a strategy in place. If you try to shortcut this process, you may see quick results in terms of numbers, but it will likely cost you later in engagement.

I once had someone send me a message on LinkedIn to ask for my LinkedIn strategy coaching support. This person was a man and had over 10,000 connections on LinkedIn, so not the usual candidate to approach me for my services on both counts.

Our conversation went something like this:

> *Person: I noticed you're a LinkedIn visibility coach. I could really do with increasing my visibility. You got any tips?*

> *Me: With 10K+ connections, I doubt you need help raising your visibility!*

> *Person: You'd be surprised! I only get around 100 views on my posts. Not sure why?*

> *Me: That is odd with so many connections. Did you grow your platform organically or with AI (artificial intelligence) help?*

> **Person:** *I added the people myself but went through a crazy phase of adding about a hundred people per day and not following up with messages. Could this be why?*

> **Me:** *The hundred – random – people a day part, likely yes. The not following up with messages, less likely.*

I had a look at this person's posts and just like he said, the average engagement per post was less than 20 likes and 5 comments.

Now these numbers are not bad in themselves if you have a small network of less than 500 people, but when you have over 10,000 people in your network and you're only getting this level of engagement on a regular basis, something is definitely wrong.

This kind of scenario tends to play out when you grow your network artificially either through an AI automation tool that randomly adds people to your network, or you've manually added random people to your network as this person had done.

Whichever way you got here, the result is the same – you have quantity, but not quality. You have a large group of people who have no interest in you or your services and therefore no reason to engage. In fact, the majority of these people are likely to be inactive – people who set up LinkedIn profiles only for them to gather dust when they check in on them every now and again.

This is not the path you want to take to grow your network. Take the "narrow road" of growing slowly and intentionally, using the 60-20-20 principle.

HOW TO **ACTIVELY** GROW YOUR LINKEDIN NETWORK

There are passive ways to grow your network on LinkedIn and active ways.

The top passive way is to write an excellent profile and optimise your profile so that you can be found in search engines and when you do get found, people actually want to connect with you from what they read about you!

If you want to actively grow your network however, there are some actions you need to take, and the first of that is to commit to adding people on a daily basis.

Adding people daily is an essential part of your business building activity on LinkedIn. You should aim to actively add people daily, especially if you currently have a small network of less than 1,000 connections.

Set realistic monthly growth goals and divide these into weeks and days to spread the load. A minimum of 10 active connections a day is a good place to start without it being too laborious or time-consuming. You can then build up gradually over time.

Here are other strategies to actively grow your network organically:

Import your email contacts

If you already have an account set up on LinkedIn, chances are you've already taken the step of importing your email contacts as suggested by LinkedIn. This is the easiest way to start growing your network organically as everyone on that list is likely to be someone you've made some kind of connection with at some point.

This is not the time to be overly fussy and selective. I've had people say to me, "I don't want to add this person from my old school because I don't want them knowing about my life." Here's a newsflash, LinkedIn is not Facebook! Your professional life is different from your personal life. These days there's not much about you that can't be discovered through an intentional Google search, so you might as well control the narrative.

In this early stage you need some building ground to work on and adding people already in your circle is a good way to start. There's nothing stopping you from removing them later on when your network gets bigger if you really want to do that. But in the beginning people like to be connected to people who already have connections – it's that same thing that tends to happen in the job market. The jobseekers who already have jobs are more desirable than those who are un-employed.

The downside to this method is that a lot of the contacts you add this way might be inactive. Lots of people set up Linked-In profiles and then leave them to gather dust, so bear this is mind in your expectations.

Add everyone you meet in real life

Ditch your business cards and get into the habit of asking everyone you meet in real life to connect with you on Linked-In, if you've decided that this is going to be your main plat-form to focus your business building (and you should con-sider making this decision, by the way. Don't spread yourself out across all the platforms – it's much better to choose one and stay faithful to it for a season, at the very least, to gain some traction and start seeing results).

You don't have to restrict it to people you meet in a professional context, add friends, neighbours, your local shopkeeper, even your gardener if need be! Sometimes our best opportunities come from our "weak ties" – people we know loosely – so be open.

Connect with active people in your feed

When you're connecting, you want to be connecting with people who are active on LinkedIn. You'll know this by looking at the activity section of their profile. Anyone who has no activity on their feed clearly isn't active. Anyone who hasn't posted or engaged with other people's content in about a fortnight or so also isn't likely to be very active.

Inviting inactive users to your network isn't useful for two reasons: 1) they're likely to not accept your request, as they won't have seen it anyway; 2) if you do get accepted and you have a lot of inactive people on your network, it has a knock-on effect on your engagement levels – i.e. there will be little to no interaction on your posts.

A NOTE ON UNACCEPTED CONNECTION INVITATIONS

Don't be tempted to send out 100 connection invitations a day in a bid to grow your network fast. LinkedIn frowns upon this kind of behaviour, and if you get too many unaccepted invitations, they will penalise you for it by temporarily restricting your account from sending invitations. You're better off gradually adding people, sticking to a maximum of 20 or so connection invitations per day.

It's good to get in the habit of clearing your sent connection invitations every so often. If you're actively adding people to grow your network, a good way to keep this in check is by deleting anyone who hasn't responded to your connection invitation after about a fortnight. At the time of writing, you can find the "withdraw invitation" setting under "manage invitations" and then clicking the sent box.

Post regularly and add anyone who likes or comments on your posts

When you start posting regularly and posting content that is attractive to your target audience and interesting to your network at large, your own profile page starts to become a magnet for attracting people to your network.

You can then take this opportunity to reach out to anyone who comments on or reacts to your posts by asking them to join your network (using a personalised message of course).

Connect with anyone who likes your comments on other people's posts

In the same vein, as you get more active on LinkedIn and strategically seek to engage with your network by adding meaningful comments on relevant posts, you'll find that other people will be drawn to you through those comments by reacting positively and/or viewing your profile. Connect with anyone who likes your comments here.

Also, read other people's comments on posts you've found interesting enough to engage with and connect with anyone here who fits the mould of your 60-20-20 profile.

Add relevant people who view your profile

If you have a regular free account, LinkedIn allows you to see up to five people at a time who's viewed your profile (a premium account is unlimited) and sends you notifications for this. Regularly look at the people that are viewing your profile and if any of them are interesting to you, and/or within your target audience, reach out and connect with them. Chances are they are likely to accept since they initiated the process (albeit unknowingly) by viewing your profile in the first place.

Connect with active members in active groups you're part of

At the time of writing, LinkedIn groups are generally dead. Dead in that most of them are un-moderated and the only activity that happens there are spammers and so-called marketing professionals trying to sell their stuff or share links nobody's interested in.

This is such a shame since the groups feature on LinkedIn was once a great way to engage with the platform and meet new people with similar interests. Many people, myself included, are holding out hope that LinkedIn does something to resurrect groups soon (this will also stop people heading over to Facebook to create and moderate groups that should rightfully be based on LinkedIn).

However, if you do find the gold dust that is a useful, active and engaged LinkedIn group within your field of interest or relating to your target audience, participate fully in this group and use it as a source to connect with active members (those that are posting or engaging regularly within the groups).

Accept almost all invitation requests

As you start being more visible on LinkedIn, you will find that connection requests will start coming your way on a regular basis. Feel free to accept almost all of these (the last 20 of your 60-20-20 strategy) but you might want to give the spammers, bitcoin and cryptocurrency sellers and the likes a miss as they'll very likely immediately hit you with an unwarranted sales pitch upon connection.

PERSONALISE YOUR CONNECTION REQUESTS

There are two good reasons to add a personal message with your connection requests. The first is because it significantly increases your acceptance rate for the most part. When you send a message with a connection request, it takes the guesswork away from the person at the other end. They no longer have to try and figure out from your profile why you want to connect with them and make a decision as to whether to oblige or not, they can just click accept (or not) because you've spelled out your intentions.

The second reason is because it's a good way to track the response from the different audiences (60-20-20) you're reaching out to and it allows you to start conversations easier (see below) since the message you send with your request is automatically posted in your inbox once they accept.

There's no need to write long paragraphs with your personalised requests. A few lines stating what attracted you to their profile and why you'd like to connect is enough. You can create templates from this that you use over and over again to save time, but be sure to always personalise the first name for that necessary personal touch.

DON'T JUST ADD PEOPLE, START CONVERSATIONS

The goal of growing your LinkedIn network is not to have an inflated network full of hundreds or even thousands of people that you don't know. The goal is to try and get to know as many of the people in your network as possible and the best way to do that is by starting conversations.

You can start conversations with your target audience through your posts, through their posts and through inbox messaging. Look for opportunities to have public conversations on posts that lead to private follow-up conversations in your inbox and then, ultimately, you want to take these conversations offline into a sales or 'discovery' call when it naturally leads to this.

Don't start conversations with the motive of trying to sell to people and definitely don't go in with a sales pitch either. People love to buy but they don't like being sold to. Instead focus on having genuine no-agenda conversations with people. Develop a curiosity and an interest in the people in your network and take your time to build meaningful relationships as much as possible.

TAKING THINGS OFFLINE

If you follow the advice in this book and you get to the place where your strategy is working well, you will find that you will start to receive messages in your inbox on a regular basis from potential clients who want to discuss working with you.

If you don't already do sales calls or discovery calls, where you have free no-obligation conversations with potential clients, start implementing these today. These calls are essential to growing your business and should be happening on a weekly basis, especially if you're still in the foundational stages of your business.

Don't rush to get someone on the phone, unless they specifically request it. Let the conversation naturally get to the place where it's easier to talk than to type before you make the suggestion.

You can also make specific offers on your posts and add a call to action that require people to sign up for a phone call with you. For example, I occasionally offer free profile review calls or free LinkedIn strategy calls on my posts to generate more sales calls when my calendar is looking a little light.

I pre-qualify the audience first by stating a strict criteria on the post (for example, I would say get in touch if you're a *woman* with a *service-based* business), and then through a questionnaire they have to complete prior to scheduling the call with me. I suggest you implement your own pre-qualification process, otherwise you'll be inundated with enquiries from people who just like taking advantage of free offers and have no interest in paying for your services.

Some of these free calls immediately convert to clients; others are fed into my mailing list for further nurturing, but *all* of them provide me with essential market research to keep on top of the pain points of my target audience.

CONCLUSION

START BEING VISIBLE ...ELSEWHERE

LINKEDIN IS A GREAT PLACE FOR YOU to start your journey to being more visible, but you don't have to end it there.

You can also apply some of these visibility techniques on other social media platforms (though they'll have their own rules you'll need to become familiar with), but I recommend only doing this once you've been consistent on LinkedIn for at least a period of time.

Even then you can consider choosing one or two other platforms to mainly focus on. Any more than that and you might be diluting your efforts and wasting your time and energy unnecessarily.

Outside of social media, other avenues of visibility to consider including starting a podcast or appearing on one as a guest, writing a book (books are excellent for visibility!), and PR strategies such as contributing to media articles or features as an expert in your field.

The possibilities are truly unlimited – but your time is not, so choose carefully!

Much love & blessings,

Mildred

NEXT STEPS

DISCOVER YOUR LINKEDIN VISIBILITY SCORE

and INCREASE your ability to elevate your brand, thought leadership and influence on LinkedIn.

The LinkedIn Visibility Scorecard is designed to measure how visible you are on LinkedIn based on the four pillars of LinkedIn success, outlined in this book (Profile, Content, Engagement and Audience).

Take the free test and receive a customised report with feedback to help you improve your LinkedIn visibility.

VISIT
StartBeingVisible.com
▲ TO START THE TEST

Ready to start being visible?

ENROL IN THE 8 WEEKS TO VISIBLE ONLINE PROGRAMME

If you want to accelerate your growth and reach your LinkedIn visibility goals faster, the 8 Weeks to Visible online programme is for you.

This programme is designed to help you implement everything you've learnt in this book about how to build a visible brand and business on LinkedIn.

Plus, you get lifetime access to our private LinkedIn community where you'll get to network with other students and graduates of the 8 Weeks programme who are also on their own journey to being visible on LinkedIn.

VISIT

StartBeingVisible.com/8weeks

TO FIND OUT MORE

Want more LinkedIn
strategies and resources?

SIGN UP TO THE START BEING VISIBLE WEEKLY NEWSLETTER

The Start Being Visible newsletter is a free weekly newsletter to help you make better use of LinkedIn for your business and personal brand.

You will get Mildred's LinkedIn strategies and resources in your inbox every week, alongside some mindset shifts to challenge your thinking, and motivation and inspiration to keep you going in those days when you feel like packing it all in.

VISIT
StartBeingVisible.com/newsletter
TO SIGN UP

ENJOYED THIS BOOK?

Please spread the word by doing one or both of these two things:

1

Leave a 5-star review on Amazon explaining what you liked about the book.

2

Share your thoughts on the book and tag Mildred on LinkedIn (**linkedin.com/in/mildredtalabi**) and/or on other social media platforms (**@mildredtalabi**).

If you include a photo of you holding the book, you'll win a free consultation call with Mildred to discuss your LinkedIn presence!

Email **info@mildredtalabi.com** to claim your prize.

Made in the USA
Las Vegas, NV
16 January 2023

65701552R00072